MARK MAREK'S
TWO-FISTED
MANAGEMENT

MR. HARRIS, SIR

AN ARNOLD HARRIS READ'N'LEAD MANUAL

TOPPER BOOKS
AN IMPRINT OF PHAROS BOOKS • A SCRIPPS HOWARD COMPANY
NEW YORK

Special thanks to Skip Johnson once again for getting the ball rolling and to Rich Landry for his inescapable editorial assistance. And thanks to Sarah Gillespie and Pat Redding.

This book is dedicated to my love interest, Leigh Ann, and my two subplots, Mia and Auston.

Pharos Books are available at special discounts on bulk purchases for sales promotions, premiums, fundraising or educational use. For details, contact the Special Sales Department, Pharos Books, 200 Park Avenue, New York, NY 10166. (212) 692-3976.

First published in 1990.

Marek, Mark.
  Two-fisted management: an Arnold Harris read 'n' lead manual / by Mark Marek.
  p. cm.
  ISBN 0-88687-510-2
  1. Executives—caricatures and cartoons. 2. Management—caricatures and cartoons.
3. Business—caricatures and cartoons.
I. Title.
PN6727.M24T96 1990
741.5'973—dc20   90-61722
                                                      CIP

Printed in the United States of America
TOPPER BOOKS
An Imprint of Pharos Books
A Scripps Howard Company
200 Park Avenue
New York, NY 10166

A WORD OF EXPLANATION

I fully realize that women play a crucial role in our modern economy—as unbridled spendthrifts. Just a joke—chill out! I'd just like to state that out of expediency I've used the pronoun "he" more than "she" in my descriptions of business practices in this book. This does not mean I don't believe that women can be just as capable as men in positions of corporate power. It simply means I have a very difficult time publicly acknowledging it.

DISCLAIMER

The opinions expressed in this book are the opinions of Mr. Harris and do not necessarily reflect the opinions of the publisher, or any reasonable-minded executive, for that matter.

DEDICATION

to my lovely housewife
and my two darling children,
Arnold Jr. and Arnette.

INTRODUCTION

In my many travels around the globe (first class, of course), I have discovered that there are two types of people—those who make money, and those who make lots of money. Of course, there are those who make no money, but when it comes right down to it, they don't really count, now, do they?

Likewise, there are two types of managers—those who command respect, and those who command respect and lots of money. Of course, there are those who command no respect and no money to speak of, but when it comes down to it, they get canned, so *they* don't really count.

The purpose of my book is to show how virtually *any* average weak-kneed capitalist pawn can become a ruthless, crackerjack corporate field commander and, as a result, garner lots of respect and lots of money like, well, like me for instance. You'll learn how to survive and succeed with just your own two hands (and the sweaty hands of those who work under you). I guarantee it or your money ba…well, I guarantee it.

Whether you are an aspiring supervisor or a mere cog in the wheel, you will find this book to be authoritative and authoritarian. Buy it, read it, and I'm sure you will profit from it. I know I will.

—A.H.

CHAPTER ONE:

MANAGEMENT THROUGH THE AGES; FROM THE AZTECS TO THE EXECS.

Since the dawn of recorded accounting, man has yearned to give orders. It was never enough, however, to simply bellow commands into the primal darkness; there had to be a recipient to this primordal boss-lust. And so, a system that came to be known as the employer/employee relationship was introduced into a heretofore harmonious social environment.

Fig. 1. Earliest Known Incident of Capitalist Scheming

The claim that men evolved from apes has often been hotly debated; however, with respect to the working classes, such ancestral claims are widely accepted.

Fig. 2. Evolutionary Chart of the Manager

For those who subscribe to more Christian principles, it is the view of many corporate theologians that on the Seventh Day, well into overtime, God manufactured the earth, appointing the management team of *Adam, Eve, and Sons* to oversee operations.

"...And He surveyed all that He had created and it was good. Or at least commercially viable."

The following is a brief synopsis of benchmark periods which distinguish the development of management from the barbarous, brutal tactics of long ago to the barbarous, brutal tactics of today.

CHAPTER TWO:

THE THEORY OF SUPPLY AND DEMAND

No student of business philosophy can possibly hope to scale the corporate ladder without a clear understanding of the basic tenet of *supply and demand*.

It's quite simply really. I've drawn up a concise diagram that should make this concept easily comprehensible. Study it. Cut it out. Laminate it. Put it in your wallet. Don't leave home without it. Whenever you are feeling something less than driven, take it out and recite it aloud. (California readers: make it your mantra.)

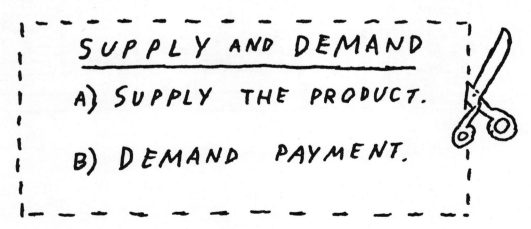

SUPPLY AND DEMAND

A) SUPPLY THE PRODUCT.

B) DEMAND PAYMENT.

Disarmingly simple? Yes. Insidiously effective? Quite. Moral? Let's move on to the next chapter, quickly now...

CHAPTER THREE:

DRESSING FOR SUCCESS

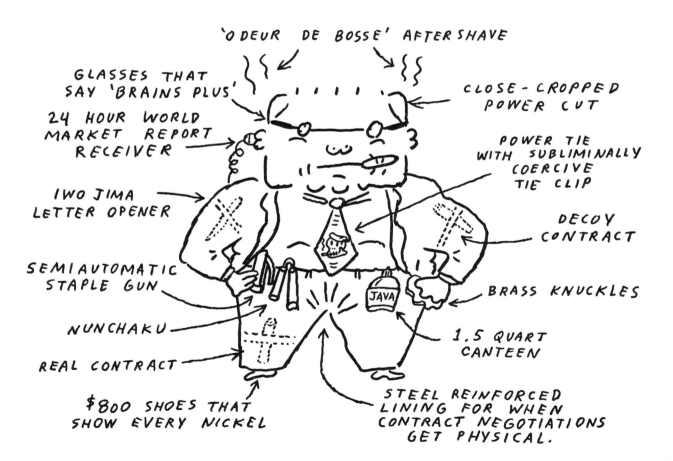

'ODEUR DE BOSSE' AFTERSHAVE

GLASSES THAT SAY 'BRAINS PLUS'

24 HOUR WORLD MARKET REPORT RECEIVER

CLOSE-CROPPED POWER CUT

POWER TIE WITH SUBLIMINALLY COERCIVE TIE CLIP

IWO JIMA LETTER OPENER

DECOY CONTRACT

SEMIAUTOMATIC STAPLE GUN

BRASS KNUCKLES

NUNCHAKU

1.5 QUART CANTEEN

REAL CONTRACT

$800 SHOES THAT SHOW EVERY NICKEL

STEEL REINFORCED LINING FOR WHEN CONTRACT NEGOTIATIONS GET PHYSICAL.

DRESSING JUST TO STAY EMPLOYED

THAT WAS THEN, THIS IS NOW; DITCH THOSE FRAMES.

DON'T EXPECT MUCH OFFICE PARTY ACTION WITH THIS 'DO'.

POSTURE? BETTER GET ONE, BUD.

WEAK CHIN; A PROMOTIONAL ROADBLOCK.

ITALIAN MARBLING SHIRT? HARDLY; TRY A HOT IRON NEXT TIME.

LACKADAISICAL TIE = LACKADAISICAL SALARY

LEATHER ELBOW PATCHES; GET WITH IT, CHAMP.

WOULD YOU TRUST A $5 MILLION DEAL WITH THESE SLACKS?

SHOES THAT WOULD BORE A TREE SLOTH

MISMATCHED SOCKS; GROUNDS FOR RELOCATION OUT OF STATE.

LOOSEN UP WITH THE MAKEUP, LADIES. COULD MAKE ALL THE DIFFERENCE BETWEEN A SURE DEAL AND A SURE DEAL WITH A PINCH ON THE BEHIND.

THIS HAIRSTYLE WENT OUT WITH THE BRADY BUNCH (CAME BACK WITH THE BRADY BUNCH, TOO).

FRILL COLLAR; GREAT IF YOU'RE AGING PREMATURELY.

MA KETTLE WAISTLINE; HIT THE EXERCYCLE, GAL.

MORE FRILLS — ENOUGH ALREADY.

HEMLINES AND EQUIVALENT SALARY LEVELS

$50,000 + PERKS, BONUSES, FREE DINNERS
$30,000
$20,000

IT'S BEEN PROVEN: SALARIES RISE IN PROPORTION TO HEELS. (QUITE THE OPPOSITE FOR MEN)

THE WELL-EQUIPPED OFFICE

A manager's office is his castle. And if that includes a moat, all the better. Herewith, my blueprint for a workplace designed to provide the around-the-clock security today's CEOs need to carry on in an increasingly hostile corporate environment:

CHAPTER FOUR:

YOU AND THE CHART

It's one thing to spout information at a board meeting but quite another thing entirely to present information without a compelling chart behind you. A chart is one of the most persuasive tools available for presenting the corporate half-truths and sundry points of propaganda which normally come up at meetings. A chart says, "Check out these bright orange profit margins." A chart says, "I have an art department and I'm not afraid to use it."

Clearly, the manager with the chart speaks more convincingly. "There are many who will doubt a manager, few who will doubt a chart." (Quote 303; please memorize.)

There are several different types of charts. A little planning beforehand will help in selecting the one appropriate to your needs.

CHARTS OF THE FUTURE:

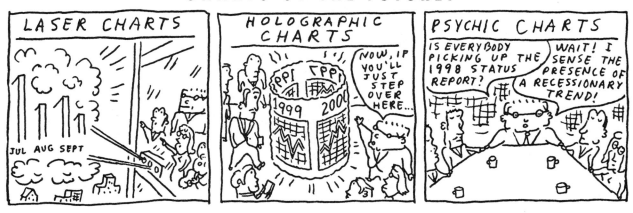

PRESENTATIONS

It's important to have your facts, figures, and bald-faced lies in order before your presentation. Organization ultimately leads to confidence which, in turn, leads to cockiness which leads to shiftiness and finagling and an all-around successful presentation.

Finally, if you feel your presentation slipping away uncontrollably, you have two last options:

CHAPTER FIVE:

PROPER DIET

A corporation is very much like the human body: the manager represents the head and the office staff constitutes the torso. Continuing with this analogy, union slackoffs would account for the fatty love-handles, while below them all would be the sales department, corresponding to...well, I think you get the idea.

The company's capital assets must be fed. Likewise, our bodies require nourishment as well.

It is a manager's responsibility to assure that one's employees are well fed. I often find it helpful to join the troops in the commissary from time to time.

With today's crazy work schedules, one has to be flexible with one's diet. You never know when you'll find yourself stranded in some deli-forsaken part of the city and have to resort to basic survivalist foraging skills:

To aid you in planning a proper diet, I've outlined some of the more common activities and their corresponding nutritional requirements.

ACTIVITY	CALORIC REQUIREMENTS	SUGGESTED DISH
MERGERS / MARATHON CONTRACT NEGOTIATIONS	280,000 cal.	PASTA, LOTS OF PASTA
HOSTILE BUYOUTS / TAKEOVERS (SUCCESSFUL)	100,000 cal.	DRINKS ALL AROUND
HOSTILE BUYOUTS / TAKEOVERS (UNSUCCESSFUL)	50,000 cal.	CRACKERS AND WATER
LABOR NEGOTIATIONS	200,000 cal.	BEEF JERKY, STALE COFFEE, CIGAR BUTTS
HIGH PRESSURE PRESENTATIONS	250,000 cal.	MEGA DOSES OF CHERRY TWIBBLES (FOR QUICK-RELEASE ENERGY).
TAX AUDITS	500,000+ cal.	ANYTHING THAT'LL STAY DOWN

THE POWER LUNCH

CHAPTER SIX:

BASIC TRAINING

Someone once said, "You learn from your mistakes." He doesn't work here any more. Sure, mistakes happen in business. So do layoffs, demotions, and salary adjustments.

Some of you may be having second thoughts about my training methods at this point. Maybe you've realized that you're just not cut out for this. Fine. Better to back out now rather than later, out there in the field, when a squad of brave, young executives will be looking to you for leadership.

If you've got no stomach for the sight of careers shattered beyond recognition or the stench of bodies beaten, burned, and left for unemployed, then I suggest you hightail it back to one of those predictably dull socialist economies. However, if you long to fight and win and bathe in the glory of fat bonus checks, then you're ready for my basic training program. Fall in line!

FIRST, A REGULATION CUT.

Let's run through an average day. Pay special attention to my consistently goal-oriented, tirelessly driven, ever so flint-hearted technique. And that's just at the Mini-Mart.

Your employees represent the company not only by their work but by their personal appearances as well. I recommend a daily morning inspection as a way to keep your staff looking sharp and feeling paranoid.

The days when deal-making involved a simple handshake and a few payoffs are over. Nowadays you'd better have your chops together. It's a no-holds-barred, watch-your-groin, tag team free-for-all out there. Expect no mercy. Show no mercy.

Once you go to the mat with the other guy, it's just you and him out there. Ok, maybe him and his accountant, but accountants are a piece of cake—one short jab to the calculator and they're out for the count.

I will now illustrate some basic offensive moves designed to take out the other guy quickly and cleanly. Then we'll study some moves designed to take him out slowly and agonizingly.

FIRST SOME FUNDAMENTAL BODY POSITIONS:

"ANCIENT OPEN-FIST, BURNING ULCER POSITION"

"THREE - FINGER CAREER CHOKE POSITION"

"YOU'RE FIRED, END-OF-DISCUSSION POSITION"

"COILED COBRA CAFFEINE-FIX POSITION"

"MONKEY BREATH GO-TO-HELL POSITION"

"DOUBLE REVERSE BUTT KICK POSITION"

A STANDARD MANEUVER, STEP-BY-STEP:

1. Maintain assertive eye contact with opponent at all times; many a contract has been won ere a bid thrown. I might suggest, for added effect, a subtly psychotic muscle twitch near the corner of the mouth—an unnerving little trick.
2. Let him throw out the first proposal. Back off—draw his weight towards you.

3. Counter with your own proposal, blocking his contract with a sweetened incentive package.
4. Before he can recover, lay down a hefty cash pledge.
5. A quick blow to the windpipe and you're outta there.

At times it may become necessary to resort to less-than-orthodox tactics. Some people would even go so far as to call them "lowdown and dirty." I'd go that far too.

Women: Should you resort to hair-pulling, be alert to the possibility of wigs or hairweaves.

Just remember: everyone is out to nail the other guy. At least, I like to think so.

NOW, HERE IS THE REQUISITION SHEET I FAXED TO YOU SOME MONTHS BACK. I BELIEVE IT'S REASONABLE; DELIVERY BY THE 25$\underline{th}$, OF COURSE.

HO HO HO

HO, HO! I WAS EXPECTING THIS. FORTUNATELY, I'VE HAD MY ELVES PUT TOGETHER A COUNTERPROPOSAL.

JUST ONE MINUTE. I DON'T SEE THE REED BUYOUT! AND WHERE'S MY NEW R&D DEPARTMENT? CHEMCO HAS A NEW R&D DEPARTMENT AND I WANT ONE TOO. I'VE BEEN A GOOD CEO ALL YEAR!

HO, HO, HO! LISTEN, HARRIS, I'M UNDERSTAFFED AND 15 MONTHS BEHIND PRODUCTION SCHEDULE. AND WITH THESE DEMOCRATIC REVOLUTIONS, I'VE GOT ROUTES POPPING UP ALL OVER EASTERN EUROPE.

TELL YOU WHAT I'LL DO. IF YOU'LL FORGET THE TELECOMMUNICATIONS CENTER AND THE NEW DATABASE SYSTEM AND THE PRIVATE SATELLITE, WELL, THEN...

...I'LL SEE WHAT I CAN DO ABOUT THE TRAIN SET.

DEFENSE MANEUVERS

Have you ever been in a tight situation at the office? Say you've put in a 60-hour week, you're under a lot of pressure. The contract is due in a half hour. You hear a knock at the door…instinctively you swivel to see who's there and find yourself looking down the business end of a loaded staple gun. How would you react? It could be an ally—perhaps a secretary. *Or it could be the enemy!* Would your reflexes be sharp enough to disarm the intruder or avoid injuring an associate?

The following drills, which can be practiced right in your office, have been designed to develop your coordination and sense of timing:

SOME OF THE MORE EFFECTIVE DEFENSIVE STRATEGIES:

THE ANTI-TAKEOVER BLOCKADE

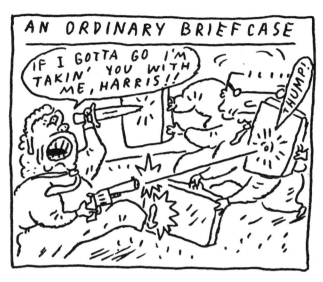

AN ORDINARY BRIEFCASE

THE INFLATABLE DECOY

A 280 LB. LAWYER

FIRST AID

I'm not gonna sit here and tell you it's a stroll through the park out there. It's not. I've seen what can happen and it's not pretty.

Now, I don't like to see an injured employee any more than the next manager. Well, maybe just a little bit more. But, the point is, injuries will occur, and if your partner has made a near-fatal career move, knowing how to cauterize an artery with a cigarette stub might just save someone's job.

BURNS:

MICROWAVE BURNS

HOT CHA CHA!

HOW MANY TIMES HAVE YOU SEEN THIS ONE? THERE'S VERY LITTLE YOU CAN DO TO ALLEVIATE THE PAIN. TRY DISTRACTING THE POOR DEVIL WITH A HEAVIER-THAN-USUAL WORK LOAD.

COFFEE BURNS

YOW! IF NOTHING ELSE IS HANDY, TWINKIES MAKE AN EXCELLENT ABSORBANT AND THE CREAM FILLING ACTS AS AN EFFECTIVE SALVE.

HEART BURN

IF YOU DON'T KNOW ENOUGH TO PACK AN ANTACID BY NOW I CAN'T BE BOTHERED. AS THEY SAY IN THE COMMISSARY—"EAT THE MEAT, TAKE THE HEAT."

COPIER FLASH:

STRAY STAPLE SHOTS:

SYSTEM CRASHES:

PAPER CUTS:

Most cuts are minor, requiring no more attention than you'd give a lost finger or a ruptured ulcer. In the event of a serious wound, these steps should be taken:

CPR (CONTRACT PROPOSAL RESUSCITATION):

One minute the deal is flying, the next minute it's flat on its back, the stale odor of death hanging heavily in the air. A little CPR and a breath mint will clear up the situation. I've seen contracts clinically dead for up to two hours brought back to life. But you must act swiftly—the longer you wait, the more likely they'll get wise to the sneakily dubious nature of your proposal.

MENTAL HEALTH:

Biologists acknowledge the value of stress in the human animal. Of course, there is good stress and there is bad stress. For instance, the stress that motivates you to excel, that keeps you awake during a make-or-break board meeting—this is good stress. The stress that has you chanting monosyllabic barnyard sounds in a toilet stall—this should be considered a somewhat bad stress one would do well to try to control.

A MANAGER'S JOB IS FRAUGHT WITH DANGER. BE ALERT TO THESE OTHER OCCUPATIONAL HAZARDS:

CHAPTER SEVEN:

IDENTIFYING HOSTILE FORCES

These days, with so many buyouts, mergers and acquisitions, it's not as easy as it once was distinguishing a business associate from a sworn competitor. That guy taking notes over in the corner at your recent top-level production meeting—was he one of *your* guys? Was he with sales? By golly, who *was* he with?

CAN YOU IDENTIFY THE ENEMY IN THIS GROUP?—

ANSWER: OK, OK, IT'S "E," BUT I GUARANTEE IT WON'T ALWAYS BE THIS EASY.

Company loyalties aren't what they used to be. Why, once I came home early and found my wife, yes, my wife, in the kitchen with (God, it still hurts)...a *Town and Suburb* magazine. The same *Town and Suburb* publication that continues to sell advertising space to *Humho Motors*—the very same *Humho Motors* that buys its aluminum-alloy engine parts from *BLT Industries,* a company whose senior CEO once snubbed me at a boat show. I mean, if you can't trust your own wife, then who can you trust?

With so many hazy distinctions, how does one spot an adversary? Well, for one thing, a person can tell a lot from a handshake:

The common necktie is a widely-used subversive tool. One should be acquainted with these symbols:

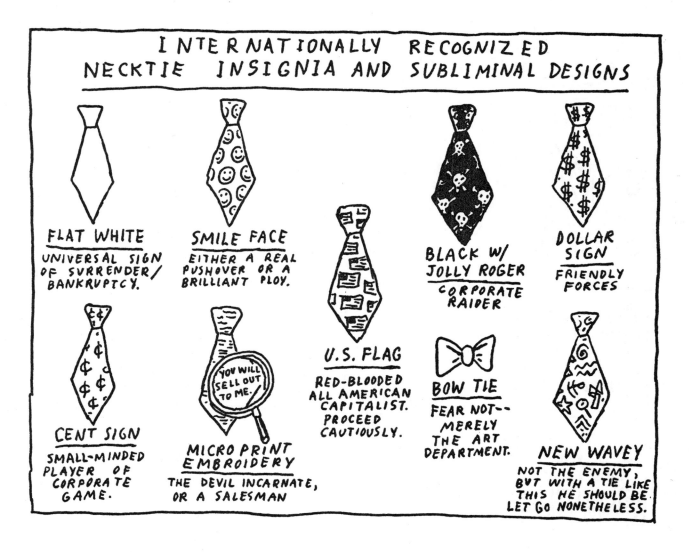

INTERNATIONALLY RECOGNIZED NECKTIE INSIGNIA AND SUBLIMINAL DESIGNS

FLAT WHITE
UNIVERSAL SIGN OF SURRENDER/ BANKRUPTCY.

SMILE FACE
EITHER A REAL PUSHOVER OR A BRILLIANT PLOY.

BLACK W/ JOLLY ROGER
CORPORATE RAIDER

DOLLAR SIGN
FRIENDLY FORCES

CENT SIGN
SMALL-MINDED PLAYER OF CORPORATE GAME.

MICRO PRINT EMBROIDERY
YOU WILL SELL OUT TO ME.
THE DEVIL INCARNATE, OR A SALESMAN

U.S. FLAG
RED-BLOODED ALL AMERICAN CAPITALIST. PROCEED CAUTIOUSLY.

BOW TIE
FEAR NOT-- MERELY THE ART DEPARTMENT.

NEW WAVEY
NOT THE ENEMY, BUT WITH A TIE LIKE THIS HE SHOULD BE. LET GO NONETHELESS.

Of course, these insignia apply as well to ties worn by women, but then I'm always suspicious of women who wear ties.

There is no end to the competitive treachery in today's business world. Fortunately. On the other hand, there is the need for constant vigilance against corporate infiltration. Double executives, if you will.

If I may quote from the Old Testament, "You gotta hit 'em hard and hit 'em where it hurts." Oh—no. Wait…excuse me, I'm looking at a CIA training manual. I always get those two books confused.

At any rate, it's still sound advice. Once you can identify the enemy, it's only good business sense to find out more about him—and his weak points.

CHAPTER EIGHT:

BATTLE STATIONS!

This is it! What you've all been waiting for. The enemy has been targeted; battle plans have been laid. It's time to rock 'n' roll!

LEADERSHIP

Some of us are born to lead and some of us are born to be led. It comes from deep within, an instinctive force that seems to say (almost out loud), "You are the anointed one, the one chosen from the midst of many to lead the many whilst squashing those who would stand in your way." In fact, some CEOs *do* hear these voices but I'd stay a few feet back from them.

If you're one of those special men and women who want to call the shots and wear the pants, then maybe you're a leader, or maybe your hormonal level is screwed up. OK, I know—I'm old-fashioned. So sue me. Either way, you know the only one you can count on is numero uno. Take, for instance, an element as unpredictable as mass transit:

AIRLINE STORMING AND BOARDING

Ah, the heady days of high-stake mergers and bloody buyouts are fast fading. Back in the early days, when modern deceptive business practices were just beginning to evolve, when men were men and women were just secretaries—now *then* I had a topnotch team of professionals working with me.

Old Blood'n'Bonus McAdams—what a CEO! He could enter a packed, hostile boardroom completely unarmed, no briefcase, no contract preparation, and twelve minutes later he'd leave with a deal signed, sealed, and tucked in his back pocket.

Then there was Ironman Wolefsky. Heh, heh; he loved to pass out commendations printed on pink slips. God, I sure do miss that jokester. He took a bad hit in the crash of '87. Yep, lost a good man or two in that one.

Well, if you'll allow this old warrior a chance to indulge, I'd like to recall one particularly rousing campaign...

THE SEVEN-DAY BIDDING WAR OF '84

WARNING:

SOME OF THE FOLLOWING FOOTAGE CONTAINS SCENES OF GRAPHIC DIVESTITURE. READER DISCRETION ADVISED.

WE JOIN THE CONFLICT IN ITS 3rd DAY OF HEATED EXCHANGE.

YA WANT 100 MILLION?! YEH!! YOU'LL HAFTA COME AND GET IT!!

ZING

POW

RAT-TAT

COVER ME, HARRY!

CLIK SNAP

(PUFF, PUFF) MS. VERNER, GET AHOLD OF OUR ACCOUNTANT. TELL HIM WE NEED ANOTHER 20 MILL'.

HE SAYS WE'VE USED UP ALL OUR RESOURCES; WE'RE ON OUR OWN.

FRANKLY, I'M SCARED!

POP!
POP!

DAY 6: THIS WAITING, THIS ENDLESS WAITING! I TELL YOU, HARRIS, I'M GONNA CRACK!!

CHAPTER NINE:

TEAMWORK

When you play the corporate game, you play to win. Not to show a negative growth rate. Not to lose clients to an overseas market. You play to win. Because no one likes a loser. The stockholders don't like a loser. Your fellow employees don't like a loser. Your two cute little preschool-age children who look up to you as such a pivotal role model—they despise a loser. The only one who likes a loser is the winner (quote #405, please memorize by tomorrow).

And just what is winning? Oh, about a 70-to-75% increase in first-quarter earnings— I'd call that winning.

MONEY ISN'T EVERYTHING; IT'S THE ONLY THING.

It takes a leader to win. Someone who can mold a group of greenhorn, third-string temp workers into a hardened, market-analyzing, tax-evading team. And that's the key word. No, not "tax-evading"—*team.*"

CHAPTER TEN:

DRUGS IN THE WORKPLACE

It has been estimated that perhaps a quarter to a third of the American workforce relies on drugs in some form to get through the average workday. The rest? I'm not sure *how* they make it through the day.

Myself, I'm rather old-fashioned on the subject. I simply don't believe in using drugs. I'm totally against them. They're destroying our families and our country—pitting father against son, black against white, CEO against general manager.

Now, before you start sizing me up as some prudish old coot, I'll have to admit I might indulge in a couple shots of J.D. before a big board meeting; maybe a couple more shots afterward to celebrate (or sulk, whichever), and when I get home I can usually polish off a fifth of Old Grandad. But drugs? That's where I draw the line. I just might not be able to walk it.

It's a manager's right and duty to take whatever steps are necessary to rout the workplace of the vile drug menace:

Half the battle is admitting there is a problem.

Once detected, it's best to ease off the drugs slowly.

CHAPTER ELEVEN:

**FORGET ABOUT IT.
NOT IN MY BOOK.**

CHAPTER TWELVE

HIRING, FIRING, AND
FORCIBLY RETIRING

The office staff is the wellspring from which a successful business doth flow. However, selecting a snappy, hardworking group of subservient drones is no simple task. It is of paramount importance to know just how to select a staff and, if need be, how to reselect a staff.

As a manager you must be able to control your employees, but to do that you must first know your employees inside and out, as distasteful as that may be.

The average employee is an uncomplicated creature, an animal driven by simple desires for money and possessions—admirable desires to be sure.

So why is it that some employees will excel while others stagnate at a particular level?

Well, thanks to improved technology, current research has revealed a bounty of new, unbiased information to help broaden our understanding of the working stiff.

Several factors seem to play a part in the overall makeup of the office worker, determining whether that person will one day manage his own department or whether his destiny will more closely follow that of the common garden slug:

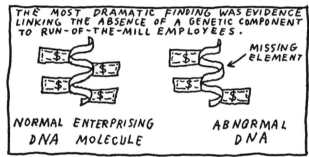

In spite of these findings, to correct this defect would only threaten the delicate biological balance that exists in the workplace. After all, if everyone was a manager, there'd be no one left to get all the work done. And if everyone was a common laborer, there'd be no one left to reap the undeserved financial rewards.

As successful manager is one who not only knows the names of every employee but also knows which name goes with which employee. As I have mentioned previously, this is not as easy as it sounds. Since electronic tagging is constitutionally out of the question, one must resort to other methods for distinguishing employees and employee types.

"Why bother?" you may ask, "As long as the work gets done, why should I care about them as individuals?"

It's a very good question and one not easily answered. Let me just say that if you are able to recognize the various types of employees, you will be far better equipped to manipulate their jobs and futures—their very lives. I suppose that's reason enough.

Also, you'll be better able to match up your employees to job positions. Just as there is the right man for the right woman, there is the right worker for the right job. The fact that you married the *wrong* person probably says a lot about your current employment situation, as well.

Let us now match some of the general employee types with appropriate jobs:

QUIET, NERVOUS, SKINNY TYPES. THE KIND WHO BUY THEIR SUITS AT SHORT AND SCRAWNY MAN'S SHOPPE.

NO JOB TOO SMALL. THEY KNOW THE VALUE OF MINIMUM WAGE. GRAB AS MANY OF THESE AS YOU CAN.

LOUD, BRASSY, FAST-TALKER TYPES. NO TALENT TO SPEAK OF AND NOT ENOUGH MONEY TO RUN FOR POLITICAL OFFICE.

PUT 'ER THERE.

SALES DEPT.

ATHLETIC JOCK TYPES WITH RED SUSPENDERS.

WHO KNOWS WHAT IN GOD'S NAME THEY DO BUT YOU'RE NOT REALLY A BUSINESS UNLESS YOU HAVE A DOZEN OR SO OF THESE MILLING ABOUT THE OFFICE.

BALDING, OVERWEIGHT TYPES WITH GLASSES.

ACCOUNTING DEPT.

BALDING, OVERWEIGHT TYPES W/OUT GLASSES.

LEGAL DEPT.

ECCENTRIC DRESSER TYPES.

ART DEPT.

INTELLIGENT, ARTICULATE, ATTRACTIVE, FEMALE TYPES.

WITH ALL THE DAMNED ERA AND GOVERNMENT INTERFERENCE YOU HAVE LITTLE CHOICE BUT TO GIVE THEM A GOOD PAYING EXECUTIVE POSITION COMMENSURATE WITH THEIR QUALIFICATIONS.

VACANT, INARTICULATE, ATTRACTIVE, FEMALE TYPES.

THERE MUST BE SOMETHING AROUND THE OFFICE FOR THEM.

YOUNG, SMART, HUNGRY, LADDER CLIMBING TYPES.

DANGEROUS! NOTHING BUT TROUBLE. THROW 'EM BACK.

INTERVIEWING

A manager must also know how to interrogate, er, *interview* prospective employees.
I would suggest a room especially designed for this purpose.

Keep the questions short and concise, and nosy. Something along the lines of:

"Who sent you?"

"Where were you on the night of the '87 crash?"

"Have you ever knowingly and willfully claimed a sick day when in fact you were out on the links?"

As for lie detectors, they are distasteful, inaccurate, unfair, and a violation of accepted hiring practices.
I use them regularly.

When it comes to salary negotiations, I can recommend several approaches for arriving at a figure:

I suppose I'll catch hell for saying this, but I'm not afraid to acknowledge the difference between men and women. It's usually around $15 G's. As the French execs say, "Vive la salaire difference!"

You can call me old-fashioned. You can call me pigheaded. But if you want to work for me, you better just call me "sir."

Now, before you get on the phone with your Congresswoman, let me point out that I have many valued female employees on my staff. Why, some of my best friends are women. Just don't tell my wife.

When it comes to interviewing women, I'm the same as I am in any interviewing situation...very discriminating. I'll usually size up all of her attributes and qualifications as best I can. Then I'll read her resume:

RETIRING

From the moment we enter the workforce, the time clock ticks away. Each day we retire a bit more as we move inexorably towards the end of our careers.

The Fabled Employees' Graveyard.

The scars of a thousand board meetings take their toll over the years. We lose our ruthless edge. In our advanced years the options are few: we can retire gracefully or we can move in to some high-paying, though essentially meaningless, figurehead CEO position. For most, the only option is the former.

It is up to each manager to help make the transition easier. Personally, I've found that employees love plaques...something with gold plating. And a presentation ceremony. It's the least you can do.

That's why I do it.

The retirement presentation ceremony is a special occasion—it's very likely the last chance you'll get to humiliate that employee in front of his or her peers.

The retirement presentation ceremony is a special occasion—it's very likely the last chance you'll get to humiliate that employee in front of his or her peers.

CHAPTER THIRTEEN:

RAISES

It's inevitable. You hire someone off the street, give 'em a good job and before you know it they want more money. How's that for gratitude.

Too many managers today are afraid to stand up for their company and say, "Hey, it's *OK* to turn a windfall profit. It's *OK* to use this great, big, beautiful corporation of ours for perfectly shallow monetary ends!"

Asking for a raise is only to be expected. It's as American as apple pie. *Denying* a raise, however, is your God-blessed patriotic *duty*. This country of ours was built on the backs of managers who got on the backs of employees. And it's time for us as managers to take back what is rightfully *theirs*.

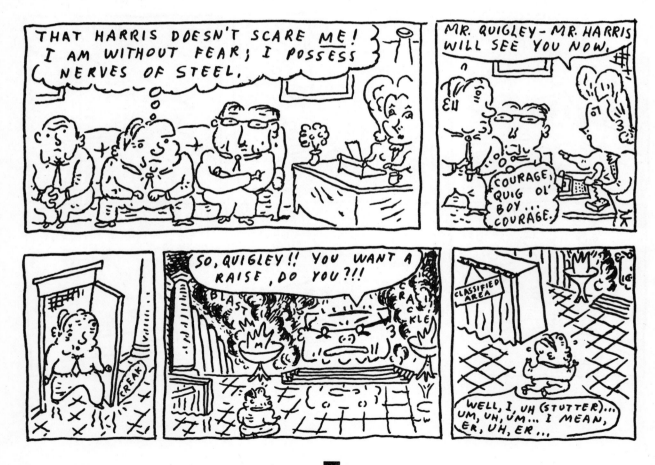

The thing to remember is that you have to compromise: if he or she asks for a 5% salary increase, you give out a 2% increase. If they ask for 10%, you give them 2%. If they ask for 15%, you settle at, oh, say 2%. That way almost everyone is happy.

CHAPTER FOURTEEN

TAXES

I've got a saying. Perhaps you've heard it: "Life's a bitch and then you pay taxes and then you die."

We capitalists get it from all sides; the church says you can't take it with you and the state says you can't have it while you're here.

Let's face it, everyone cheats on their taxes. Everyone. Maybe a little, maybe a lot. Don't get me wrong—I'm not saying it's right. No, I pay my lawyers to say that.

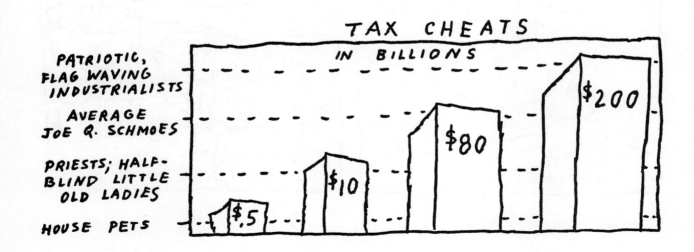

TAX CHEATS IN BILLIONS

PATRIOTIC, FLAG WAVING INDUSTRIALISTS — $200

AVERAGE JOE Q. SCHMOES — $80

PRIESTS; HALF-BLIND LITTLE OLD LADIES — $10

HOUSE PETS — $.5

Now, you can go right ahead and pay all your taxes if you want and sleep well at night and maybe even die with a clean slate, ready for that big audit in the sky. But I have a special calling in life—a mission, if you will, a sacred mission from the Boss Almighty. (Maybe that's stretching it a tad.)

At any rate, I was put on this earth for one purpose—to make excessive amounts of money. And, I've developed a few tricks along the way that have enabled me to keep well-nigh all of it. I'd like to share some of those tricks now. Perhaps then we can all get back to the good old days when life was just a bitch and then you died.

Of course we've all heard that you can't take it with you. Personally, I couldn't look at myself in the mirror each morning and feel good about calling myself a capitalist entrepreneur if I didn't try to work out some sort of afterlife arrangement.

It all boils down to a currency exchange technicality: in this life, $70,000 might buy you a lifetime 50-yard-line seat at Giant Stadium, but *Upstairs* it wouldn't get you a moldy little rain cloud.

So what can you do? Invest. That's right; set aside 5 to 10% of your income to invest in the religion of your choice. Most transactions can be conducted during church services, or you may wish to use an independent clerical broker.

Either way, you build up equity in grace, karma, what-have-you. No fuss. No muss. No unpleasant kneeling and praying. By the time you pass on, you'll have a heavenly little nest egg waiting for you. Of course, there are severe penalties for going the other way. And don't forget—hold on to your receipts.

CHAPTER FIFTEEN:

COMPANY MORALE

In this country there are three institutions which Americans hold sacred: the Family, the Church, and, of course, the Coffee Break.

Now, you could probably persuade a man to leave his wife and kids, and it wouldn't be impossible to lead a born-again Christian into a dark deed now and then, but if you've ever thought you could take away an employee's coffee break, think again.

To its credit, the coffee break does act as a safety valve to enable employees to cool off after several hours of humbling drudgery. Fine. But even this exalted little oasis can and should be controlled before it develops into a full-blown rest period.

And timer-controlled electric shock seats in the lavatories are effective with those trying to extend their break elsewhere.

THE ANNUAL PICNIC

The company that plays together, stays together. That's why I sponsor an annual picnic for my employees.

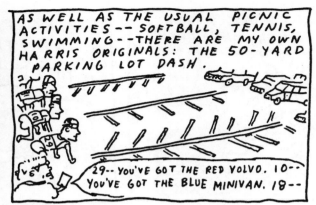

BONUSES AND PERKS

There will be times when an employee will go beyond his normal routine and actually *finish* a job. At these times, it is good business to employ a reward system (otherwise known as bonuses). Generally, bonuses are payments intended to quell feelings of exploitation and resentment that invariably build up throughout the year. There are, however, other types of bonuses than cash payments:

Sometimes it pays off to make over your employees almost as if you valued them. A bulletin board featuring employee profiles is an excellent way to boost their wretched little egos:

EMPLOYEES OF THE MONTH
(WHERE ARE THEY NOW?)

DOUG "DO IT MYSELF" MULLER (JAN. '76)

1976 — DOUG WAS THE KIND WHO ALWAYS HAD TO DO IT HIMSELF; HAD A HAND IN EVERYTHING.

TODAY — DOUG LAID HIMSELF OFF IN '83.

GLADYS DEL RIO (JUNE '78)

1978 — A RESOURCEFUL, SAVVY, BUSINESS-WOMAN. SHOO-IN FOR THE BOARD.

TODAY — THESE DAYS GLADYS HEADS UP A SLICK HIGH-POWERED FAMILY; MEMBER OF THE PTA; BROWNIE DEN MOTHER; WOMEN'S GUILD V.P.; NEIGH-BORHOOD ASSOCIATION MERGER IN THE WORKS.

JERRY SOUSSA (DEC. '81)

1981 — ACE MAIL ROOM ATTENDANT. THREE-TIME E.O.T.M.

TODAY — CURRENTLY, JERRY CONTINUES HIS FIRST-RATE JOB DOWN IN THE MAILROOM.

T K FLYNN (APRIL '86)

1986 — YOUNG, AMBITIOUS, TYPE 'A' PERSON-ALITY. WANTED IT ALL AND WANTED IT YESTERDAY.

TODAY — OLD BEFORE HIS TIME.

BERNICE MERRIWEATHER (FEB. '87)

1987 — BERNICE'S FEBRUARY WORK OUTPUT WAS HER BEST EVER. IN FACT, HER CAREER HAS DECLINED STEADILY EVER SINCE.

TODAY — LAST SEEN AT THE POTATOES-R-US FAST FOOD COUNTER AT THE MILL CREEK MALL.

LOU OGILVY (MARCH '80)

1980 — ALL AROUND DECENT SORT OF FELLOW. "FAIR AND SQUARE LOU," "MR. NICE GUY."

TODAY — FINISHED LAST.

CHAPTER SIXTEEN:

GOOD DAYS/BAD DAYS

THE DAY EVERYTHING WENT RIGHT

EVERYONE WAS AT THE OFFICE AND HARD AT WORK 19 MINUTES BEFORE MR. HARRIS.

THE PRESTIGIOUS HENDERSON ACCOUNT CAME THROUGH; WORTH IN THE NEIGHBORHOOD OF 2 MILL' IN ANNUAL BILLINGS.

COME TO PAPA!

ALL SCHEDULED MEETINGS WENT SMOOTHLY WITHOUT INTERRUPTIONS, PROVIDING SOLUTIONS TO A VARIETY OF NAGGING CORPORATE PROBLEMS.

WHAT IF WE MERGED?

THE QUARTERLY REPORT WAS RELEASED WITH A SHINING REVIEW OF PROFITS CONTAINED THEREIN.

HMM, YES, MMM... I'M LIKING THIS, YES...

A.H. INC 1991

ZEMCO, ONE HELLUVA MAJOR COMPETITOR, WENT CHAPTER ELEVEN.

YOU DON'T SAY!

NOT ONE BUT TWO BOXES OF CHERRY TWIBBLES DROPPED DOWN IN THE VENDING MACHINE!!

WILL YOU LOOK AT THAT!

KLUNK KLUNK

Every so often, even for a good manager, things get out of control; nothing gets done, everyone is on your ass, a nervous breakdown is around the corner. Now you know how your employees feel five days a week!

CHAPTER SEVENTEEN:

SPECIAL FOCUS SEGMENT
FAST FOOD MANAGERS

Who are they, why they are so crucial to our economy and why do they all look like overweight high school P.E. instructors?

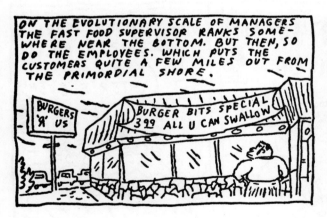

ON THE EVOLUTIONARY SCALE OF MANAGERS THE FAST FOOD SUPERVISOR RANKS SOME-WHERE NEAR THE BOTTOM. BUT THEN, SO DO THE EMPLOYEES. WHICH PUTS THE CUSTOMERS QUITE A FEW MILES OUT FROM THE PRIMORDIAL SHORE.

BURGERS 'R' US

BURGER BITS SPECIAL 3 99 ALL U CAN SWALLOW

STILL, HE SHARES SOME TRAITS WITH HIS MORE FORTUNATE CORPORATE COUSINS, LIKE BUSINESS SAVVY.

BEGLY, WE'LL RUN THE 2 FOR 1 FLUFFY MUFFIN SPECIAL THIS WEEK.

DELWOOD, PUT OFF THE TEENY TINY TOY FREEBIE. THE TIMING'S NOT RIGHT.

CHAPTER EIGHTEEN:

ADVANCED TECHNIQUES

You know, it wasn't really that long ago I used to be an average Joe, happy-to-get-my-weekly-paycheck sort of fellow. Like you. Then I realized that I was going nowhere in the company; promotions passed me by; I was earning less than the national average for managers of my caliber. Actually, my wife pointed all of this out to me.

The clincher was losing the PBO Industries contract to some skinny little runt of a guy with a degree from Brown. That's when I decided to change. I started working excessive hours and eating fast foods instead of those slower home-cooked meals, and I developed my own system of tried, tried again, and true management techniques that made me what I am today. Techniques which can make *you* what I am today. *After I retire.*

CELLULAR PHONE TECHNIQUE #82

EVEN IF YOU DON'T ACT LIKE A SAVVY, WHEELING-DEALING MANAGER, YOU CAN AT LEAST SOUND LIKE ONE. NOTHING CUTS TO THE CORE OF A BUSINESS ISSUE QUITE LIKE A COLORFUL PHRASE. HERE ARE SOME OF MY FAVORITES:

THE BUCK STARTS HERE

TELL YA WHAT, JACK, RUN IT UP THE FLAGPOLE AND SEE WHO SALUTES.

WHAT?

YOU HEARD ME; GIVE 'EM THE WHOLE BALL OF WAX.

WHAT'S THAT??

DO I HAFTA SPELL IT OUT? SELL 'EM THE WHISTLE OFF THE FACTORY. YOU KNOW, GIVE 'EM A SET OF LEFT-HANDED SCREWDRIVERS.

SAY WHAT???

CHAPTER NINETEEN:

NEW AGE MONEYGRUBBING (BUSINESS IN THE NINETIES)

After centuries of evolutionary natural selection, we have reached an unprecedented capitalist plateau. We've come a long way in understanding our cosmic interdependence. Without each person's unique inner contribution to the whole, a profit of 60 to 70% might not be possible.

DIRECT-SALES OFFICE EQUIPMENT

Call now! Underpaid operators are standing by. All profits final.

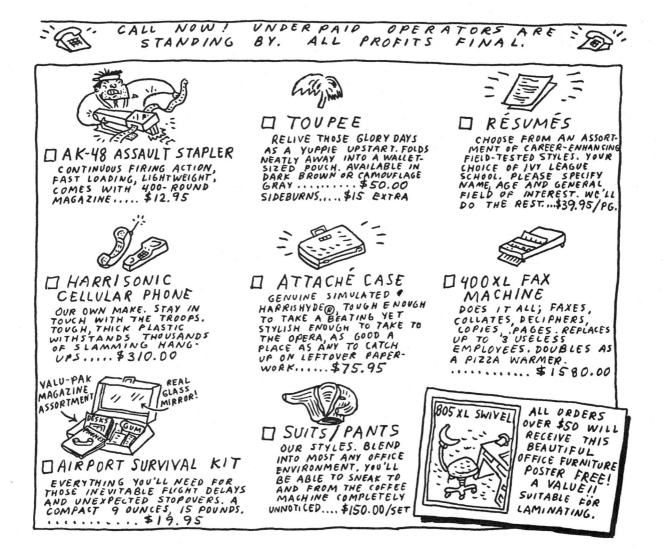

CALL NOW! UNDERPAID OPERATORS ARE STANDING BY. ALL PROFITS FINAL.

☐ **AK-48 ASSAULT STAPLER**
CONTINUOUS FIRING ACTION, FAST LOADING, LIGHTWEIGHT, COMES WITH 400-ROUND MAGAZINE..... $12.95

☐ **TOUPEE**
RELIVE THOSE GLORY DAYS AS A YUPPIE UPSTART. FOLDS NEATLY AWAY INTO A WALLET-SIZED POUCH. AVAILABLE IN DARK BROWN OR CAMOUFLAGE GRAY......... $50.00
SIDEBURNS..... $15 EXTRA

☐ **RÉSUMÉS**
CHOOSE FROM AN ASSORT-MENT OF CAREER-ENHANCING FIELD-TESTED STYLES. YOUR CHOICE OF IVY LEAGUE SCHOOL. PLEASE SPECIFY NAME, AGE AND GENERAL FIELD OF INTEREST. WE'LL DO THE REST....$39.95/PG.

☐ **HARRISONIC CELLULAR PHONE**
OUR OWN MAKE. STAY IN TOUCH WITH THE TROOPS. TOUGH, THICK PLASTIC WITHSTANDS THOUSANDS OF SLAMMING HANG-UPS..... $310.00

☐ **ATTACHÉ CASE**
GENUINE SIMULATED HARRISHYDE®, TOUGH ENOUGH TO TAKE A BEATING YET STYLISH ENOUGH TO TAKE TO THE OPERA, AS GOOD A PLACE AS ANY TO CATCH UP ON LEFTOVER PAPER-WORK...... $75.95

☐ **400XL FAX MACHINE**
DOES IT ALL; FAXES, COLLATES, DECIPHERS, COPIES, PAGES. REPLACES UP TO 3 USELESS EMPLOYEES. DOUBLES AS A PIZZA WARMER.
.... $1580.00

VALU-PAK MAGAZINE ASSORTMENT
REAL GLASS MIRROR!
DESKS GUM PHONES

☐ **AIRPORT SURVIVAL KIT**
EVERYTHING YOU'LL NEED FOR THOSE INEVITABLE FLIGHT DELAYS AND UNEXPECTED STOPOVERS. A COMPACT 9 OUNCES, 15 POUNDS.
.... $19.95

☐ **SUITS/PANTS**
OUR STYLES. BLEND INTO MOST ANY OFFICE ENVIRONMENT. YOU'LL BE ABLE TO SNEAK TO AND FROM THE COFFEE MACHINE COMPLETELY UNNOTICED.... $150.00/SET

805 XL SWIVEL
ALL ORDERS OVER $50 WILL RECEIVE THIS BEAUTIFUL OFFICE FURNITURE POSTER FREE! A VALUE!! SUITABLE FOR LAMINATING.

Tired of sitting around during your coffee break engaging in small talk with your fellow employees? Well, be bored no longer. Grab your pencils and thinking caps and get ready for hours—er, well, better keep it at 15 minutes of fun with the…

TWO-FISTED® FUN ACTIVITY PAGE

OFFICE MAZE

SEE HOW QUICKLY YOU CAN FIND YOUR WAY TO MR. HARRIS'S OFFICE. BETTER HURRY! AND TRY NOT TO RUN INTO OVERTIME!

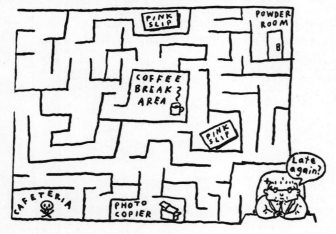

WHAT'S WRONG WITH THIS PICTURE?

ANSWERS:

A. THE SECRETARY IS SLOUCHING OFF.
B. NIGHT CLEANUP WAS LESS THAN THOROUGH WITH THE GLASS DOORS.
C. TELEPHONES ARE SILENT.
D. MR. HARRIS IS AUTHORIZING A SALARY INCREASE OF OVER 5%.

WORD SEARCH

CAN YOU FIND THE OFT-USED UPPER MANAGEMENT BUSINESS MAXIM IN THIS DIAGRAM?

```
V Z R T N A P U X
D O G E A T D O G
H C I B C F U I N
```

NOW, GET BACK TO WORK !!!